Albert Ei

Quotes & Facts

By Blago Kirov

First Edition

*****

Albert Einstein: Quotes & Facts
*****

Foreword

"Two things are infinite: the universe and human stupidity; and I'm not sure about the universe."

This book is an anthology of 238 quotes from Albert Einstein and 73 selected facts about Albert Einstein.

Albert Einstein was offered the Presidency of Israel but declined, having no political or ceremonial ambitions. Refusing the Presidency of Israel, he said, "I know a little of science, but nothing about men."
Albert Einstein is named Time magazine's Person of the Century.
Einstein did not win the 1921 Nobel Prize in Physics for his work on Relativity.
After Einstein divorced his first wife, Mileva Maric, in 1919, he married his cousin, Elsa Loewenthal (nee Einstein). Albert's mother and Elsa's mother were sisters, plus Albert's father and Elsa's father were cousins.
Einstein loved to smoke. In 1950, Einstein is noted as saying, "I believe that pipe smoking contributes to a somewhat calm and objective judgment in all human affairs," Although he favored pipes, Einstein was not one to turn down a cigar or even a cigarette.
In letters that he wrote to Elsa, Einstein readily acknowledged many extramarital affairs. He wrote that his girlfriends showered him with "unwanted" affection.
In letter to his second wife Elsa, Einstein wrote that he "got away without wearing socks" at the University of Oxford.
Albert Einstein once used a $1500.00 check as a bookmark and then lost the book.
Hitler considered Albert Einstein public enemy number one.

Charlie Chaplin told Albert Einstein: "They cheer me because they all understand me, and they cheer you because no one understands you."

"A table, a chair, a bowl of fruit and a violin; what else does a man need to be happy?"
"Any fool can know. The point is to understand."
"Creativity is intelligence having fun."
"Education is what remains after one has forgotten what one has learned in school."
"Genius is 1% talent and 99% percent hard work..."
"I have not failed; I have just found 10,000 ways that don't work."
"If you can't explain it to a six year old, you don't understand it yourself."
"In the middle of difficulty lies opportunity"
"Men marry women with the hope they will never change. Women marry men with the hope they will change. Invariably they are both disappointed."
"A clever person solves a problem. A wise person avoids it."
"A foolish faith in authority is the worst enemy of truth."

His Words

"I have no special talents. I am only passionately curious."

"A table, a chair, a bowl of fruit and a violin; what else does a man need to be happy?"

"Any fool can know. The point is to understand."

"Creativity is intelligence having fun."

"Education is what remains after one has forgotten what one has learned in school."

"Genius is 1% talent and 99% percent hard work..."

"I have not failed; I have just found 10,000 ways that don't work."

"If you can't explain it to a six year old, you don't understand it yourself."

"In the middle of difficulty lies opportunity"

"Men marry women with the hope they will never change. Women marry men with the hope they will change. Invariably they are both disappointed."

"A clever person solves a problem. A wise person avoids it."

"A foolish faith in authority is the worst enemy of truth."

"A human being is a part of the whole called by us universe, a part limited in time and space. He experiences himself, his thoughts and feeling as something separated from the rest, a kind of optical delusion of his consciousness. This delusion is a kind of prison for us, restricting us to our personal desires and to affection for a few persons nearest to us. Our task must be to free ourselves from this prison by widening our circle of compassion to embrace all living creatures and the whole of nature in its beauty."

"A little knowledge is a dangerous thing. So is a lot."

"A man should look for what is, and not for what he thinks should be."

"A perfection of means, and confusion of aims, seems to be our main problem."

"A person starts to live when he can live outside himself."

"A question that sometimes drives me hazy: am I or are the others crazy?"

"A ship is always safe at the shore - but that is NOT what it is built for."

"A society's competitive advantage will come not from how well its schools teach the multiplication and periodic tables, but from how well they stimulate imagination and creativity."

"A true genius admits that he/she knows nothing."

"All generalizations are false, including this one."

"All religions, arts and sciences are branches of the same tree. All these aspirations are directed toward ennobling man's life, lifting it from the sphere of mere physical existence and leading the individual towards freedom."

"Always do what's right; this will gratify some and astonish the rest"

"An empty stomach is not a good political adviser."

"Any man who can drive safely while kissing a pretty girl is simply not giving the kiss the attention it deserves."

"Anyone who doesn't take truth seriously in small matters cannot be trusted in large ones either."

"Anyone who has never made a mistake has never tried anything new."

"As far as the laws of mathematics refer to reality, they are not certain; and as far as they are certain, they do not refer to reality."

"As the area of light expands, so does the perimeter of darkness."

"At least once a day, allow yourself the freedom to think and dream for yourself."

"Before God we are all equally wise - and equally foolish."

"Black holes are where God divided by zero."

"Blind belief in authority is the greatest enemy of truth."

"Coincidence is God's way of remaining anonymous."

"Common sense is the collection of prejudices acquired by age eighteen."

"Common sense is what tells us the earth is flat."

"Compound interest is the eighth wonder of the world. He who understands it, earns it ... he who doesn't ... pays it."

"Creating a new theory is not like destroying an old barn and erecting a skyscraper in its place. It is rather like climbing a mountain, gaining new and wider views, discovering unexpected connections between our starting points and its rich environment. But the point from which we started out still exists and can be seen, although it appears smaller and forms a tiny part of our broad view gained by the mastery of the obstacles on our adventurous way up."

"Creativity is knowing how to hide your sources"

"Dancers are the athletes of God."

"Do not worry about your difficulties in Mathematics. I can assure you mine are still greater."

"Energy cannot be created or destroyed; it can only be changed from one form to another."

"Even on the most solemn occasions I got away without wearing socks and hid that lack of civilization in high boots"

"Everybody is a genius. But if you judge a fish by its ability to climb a tree, it will live its whole life believing that it is stupid."

"Everyone must become their own person, however frightful that may be."

"Everything is determined, the beginning as well as the end, by forces over which we have no control. It is determined for the insect, as well as for the star. Human beings, vegetables, or cosmic dust, we all dance to a mysterious tune, intoned in the distance by an invisible piper."

"Everything must be made as simple as possible. But not simpler."

"Everything that is really great and inspiring is created by the individual who can labor in freedom."

"Excellence is doing a common thing in an uncommon way."

"Failing isn't bad when you learn what not to do."

"Few are those who see with their own eyes and feel with their own hearts."

"Force always attracts men of low morality."

"From the standpoint of daily life, however, there is one thing we do know: that we are here for the sake of each other - above all for those upon whose smile and well-being our own happiness depends, and also for the countless unknown souls with whose fate we are connected by a bond of sympathy. Many times a day I realize how much my own outer and inner life is built upon the labors of my fellow men, both living and dead, and how earnestly I must exert myself in order to give in return as much as I have received."

"God did not create evil. Just as darkness is the absence of light, evil is the absence of God."

"God does not play dice with the universe."

"Few people are capable of expressing with equanimity opinions which differ from the prejudices of their social environment. Most people are incapable of forming such opinions."

"God is subtle but he is not malicious."

"Gravitation cannot be held responsible for people falling in love. How on earth can you explain in terms of chemistry and physics so important a biological phenomenon as first love? Put your hand on a stove for a minute and it seems like an hour. Sit with that special girl for an hour and it seems like a minute. That's relativity."

"Gravitation is not responsible for people falling in love."

"Great spirits have always encountered violent opposition from mediocre minds."

"He to whom this emotion is a stranger, who can no longer pause to wonder and stand rapt in awe, is as good as dead: his eyes are closed."

"How I wish that somewhere there existed an island for those who are wise and of good will."

"However rare true love may be, it is less so than true friendship."

"He who joyfully marches to music rank and file has already earned my contempt. He has been given a large brain by mistake, since for him the spinal cord would surely suffice. This disgrace to civilization should be done away with at once. Heroism at command, senseless brutality, deplorable love-of-country stance and all the loathsome nonsense that goes by the name of patriotism, how violently I hate all this, how despicable and ignoble war is; I would rather be torn to shreds than be part of so base an action! It is my conviction that killing under the cloak of war is nothing but an act of murder."

"I am enough of an artist to draw freely upon my imagination. Imagination is more important than knowledge. Knowledge is limited. Imagination encircles the world."

"I believe in intuitions and inspirations...I sometimes FEEL that I am right. I do not KNOW that I am."

"I believe that Gandhi's views were the most enlightened of all the political men in our time. We should strive to do things in his spirit: not to use violence in fighting for our cause, but by non-participation in anything you believe is evil."

"I cannot imagine a God who rewards and punishes the objects of his creation, whose purposes are modeled after our own -- a God, in short, who is but a reflection of human frailty. Neither can I believe that the individual survives the death of his body, although feeble souls harbor such thoughts through fear or ridiculous egotisms."

"I do not teach anyone I only provide the environment in which they can learn"

"I don't know, I don't care, and it doesn't make any difference!"

"I don't need to know everything; I just need to know where to find it, when I need it"

"I don't try to imagine a personal God; it suffices to stand in awe at the structure of the world, insofar as it allows our inadequate senses to appreciate it."

"I fear the day technology will surpass our human interaction. The world will have a generation of idiots."

"I know not with what weapons World War III will be fought, but World War IV will be fought with sticks and stones."

"I live in that solitude which is painful in youth, but delicious in the years of maturity."

"I love Humanity but I hate humans"

"I must be willing to give up what I am in order to become what I will be."

"I never made one of my discoveries through the process of rational thinking"

"I never teach my pupils, I only attempt to provide the conditions in which they can learn."

"I never think of the future - it comes soon enough."

"I see my life in terms of music."

"I speak to everyone in the same way, whether he is the garbage man or the president of the university."

"I thought of that while riding my bicycle."

"I want to know God's thoughts - the rest are mere
details."

"I'd rather be an optimist and a fool than a pessimist
and right."

"If a cluttered desk is a sign of a cluttered mind, of
what, then, is an empty desk a sign?"

"If A is a success in life, then A equals x plus y plus z.
Work is x; y is play; and z is keeping your mouth shut"

"If at first the idea is not absurd, then there is no hope for it."

"If I could do it all again, I'd be a plumber."

"If I had an hour to solve a problem I'd spend 55 minutes thinking about the problem and 5 minutes thinking about solutions."

"If I were not a physicist, I would probably be a musician. I often think in music. I live my daydreams in music. I see my life in terms of music."

"If I were to remain silent, I'd be guilty of complicity."

"If most of us are ashamed of shabby clothes and shoddy furniture let us be more ashamed of shabby ideas and shoddy philosophies.... It would be a sad situation if the wrapper were better than the meat wrapped inside it."

"If my theory of relativity is proven successful, Germany will claim me as a German and France will declare me a citizen of the world. Should my theory prove untrue, France will say that I am a German, and Germany will declare that I am a Jew."

"If people are good only because they fear punishment, and hope for reward, then we are a sorry lot indeed."

"If the facts don't fit the theory, change the facts."

"If there is any religion that could respond to the needs of modern science, it would be Buddhism."

"If we knew what it was we were doing, it would not be called research, would it?"

"If you don't have time to do it right, when will you have time to do it over?"

"If you want to live a happy life, tie it to a goal, not to people or things."

"If you want your children to be intelligent, read them fairy tales. If you want them to be more intelligent, read them more fairy tales."

"Imagination is everything. It is the preview of life's coming attractions."

"Imagination is more important than knowledge. For knowledge is limited to all we now know and understand, while imagination embraces the entire world, and all there ever will be to know and understand."

"Imagination is the highest form of research."

"In theory, theory and practice are the same. In practice, they are not."

"Information is not knowledge."

"Intellectual growth should commence at birth and cease only at death."

"Intelligence is not the ability to store information, but to know where to find it."

"It gives me great pleasure indeed to see the stubbornness of an incorrigible nonconformist warmly acclaimed."

"It has become appallingly obvious that our technology has exceeded our humanity."

"It is harder to crack prejudice than an atom."

"It is my conviction that killing under the cloak of war is nothing but an act of murder."

"It is my view that the vegetarian manner of living, by its purely physical effect on the human temperament, would most beneficially influence the lot of mankind."

"It is not that I'm so smart. But I stay with the questions much longer."

"It is the supreme art of the teacher to awaken joy in creative expression and knowledge."

"It is, in fact, nothing short of a miracle that the modern methods of instruction have not yet entirely strangled the holy curiosity of inquiry; for this delicate little plant, aside from stimulation, stands mainly in need of freedom. Without this it goes to wrack and ruin without fail."

"It occurred to me by intuition, and music was the driving force behind that intuition. My discovery was the result of musical perception."

"It seems to me that the idea of a personal God is an anthropological concept which I cannot take seriously. I also cannot imagine some will or goal outside the human sphere... Science has been charged with undermining morality, but the charge is unjust. A man's ethical behavior should be based effectually on sympathy, education, and social ties and needs; no religious basis is necessary. Man would indeed be in a poor way if he had to be restrained by fear of punishment and hope of reward after death."

"It would be my greatest sadness to see Zionists (Jews) do to Palestinian Arabs much of what Nazis did to Jews."

"It would be possible to describe everything scientifically, but it would make no sense; it would be without meaning, as if you described a Beethoven symphony as a variation of wave pressure."

"Laws alone can not secure freedom of expression; in order that every man present his views without penalty there must be spirit of tolerance in the entire population."

"Learn from yesterday, live for today, hope for tomorrow. The important thing is to not stop questioning."

"Learning is experience. Everything else is just information."

"Life is a preparation for the future; and the best preparation for the future is to live as if there were none."

"Life is like riding a bicycle. To keep your balance, you must keep moving."

"Life isn't worth living, unless it is lived for someone else."

"Logic will get you from A to Z; imagination will get you everywhere."

"Look deep into nature, and then you will understand everything better."

"Love is a better master than duty."

"My pacifism is an instinctive feeling, a feeling that possesses me because the murder of men is disgusting. My attitude is not derived from any intellectual theory but is based on my deepest antipathy to every kind of cruelty and hatred."

"My passionate sense of social justice and social responsibility has always contrasted oddly with my pronounced lack of need for direct contact with other human beings and human communities. I am truly a 'lone traveler' and have never belonged to my country, my home, my friends, or even my immediate family, with my whole heart; in the face of all these ties, I have never lost a sense of distance and a need for solitude... "

"My religion consists of a humble admiration of the illimitable superior spirit who reveals himself in the slight details we are able to perceive with our frail and feeble mind."

"Never do anything against conscience, even if the state demands it."

"Never memorize something that you can look up."

"No amount of experimentation can ever prove me right; a single experiment can prove me wrong."

"No, this trick won't work... How on earth are you ever going to explain in terms of chemistry and physics so important a biological phenomenon as first love? "

"Nothing happens until something moves."

"Nothing will benefit human health and increase the chances for survival of life on Earth as much as the evolution to a vegetarian diet."

"Now he has departed from this strange world a little ahead of me. That means nothing. People like us, who believe in physics, know that the distinction between past, present, and future is only a stubbornly persistent illusion."

"Older men start wars, but younger men fight them. "

"Once we accept our limits, we go beyond them."

"Once you can accept the universe as matter expanding into nothing that is something, wearing stripes with plaid comes easy."

"One cannot alter a condition with the same mind set that created it in the first place."

"One of the strongest motives that lead men to art and science is escape from everyday life with its painful crudity and hopeless dreariness, from the fetters of one's own ever-shifting desires. A finely tempered nature longs to escape from the personal life into the world of objective perception and thought."

"One thing I have learned in a long life: that all our science, measured against reality, is primitive and childlike -- and yet it is the most precious thing we have."

"Only a life lived for others is a life worthwhile."

"Only those who attempt the absurd can achieve the impossible."

"Our separation from each other is an optical illusion."

"Our task must be to free ourselves... by widening our circle of compassion to embrace all living creatures and the whole of nature and it's beauty."

"Out of clutter, find simplicity. From discord, find harmony. In the middle of difficulty lies opportunity."

"Out of clutter, find simplicity."

"Past is dead

"Peace cannot be kept by force; it can only be achieved by understanding."

"Play is the highest form of research."

"Possessions, outward success, publicity, luxury - to me these have always been contemptible. I believe that a simple and unassuming manner of life is best for everyone, best for both the body and the mind."

"Present is all you have, so eat, drink and live merry; future is uncertain"

"Pure mathematics is in its way the poetry of logical ideas."

"Reading, after a certain age, diverts the mind too much from its creative pursuits. Any man who reads too much and uses his own brain too little falls into lazy habits of thinking."

"Reality is merely an illusion, albeit a very persistent one."

"Science without religion is lame, religion without science is blind."

"Setting an example is not the main means of influencing others, it is the only means."

"Small is the number of people who see with their eyes and think with their minds"

"Solitude is painful when one is young, but delightful when one is more mature. "

"Somebody who only reads newspapers and at best books of contemporary authors looks to me like an extremely near-sighted person who scorns eyeglasses. He is completely dependent on the prejudices and fashions of his times, since he never gets to see or hear anything else."

"Strange is our situation here on Earth. Each of us comes for a short visit, not knowing why, yet sometimes seeming to divine a purpose. From the standpoint of daily life, however, there is one thing we do know: that man is here for the sake of other men - above all for those upon whose smiles and well-being our own happiness depends."

"Student is not a container you have to fill but a torch you have to light up."

"Teaching should be such that what is offered is perceived as a valuable gift and not as hard duty. Never regard study as duty but as the enviable opportunity to learn to know the liberating influence of beauty in the realm of the spirit for your own personal joy and to the profit of the community to which your later work belongs."

"The best way to cheer yourself is to cheer somebody else up."

"The bigotry of the nonbeliever is for me nearly as funny as the bigotry of the believer."

"The difference between genius and stupidity is; genius has its limits."

"The hardest thing in the world to understand is the income tax."

"The human spirit must prevail over technology."

"The ideals which have always shone before me and filled me with joy are goodness, beauty, and truth."

"The important thing is not to stop questioning. Curiosity has its own reason for existing."

"The intellect has little to do on the road to discovery. There comes a leap in consciousness, call it Intuition or what you will, the solution comes to you and you don't know how or why."
"The intuitive mind is a sacred gift and the rational mind is a faithful servant. We have created a society that honors the servant and has forgotten the gift."

"The measure of intelligence is the ability to change."

"The mind that opens to a new idea never returns to its original size."

"The most beautiful experience we can have is the mysterious - the fundamental emotion which stands at the cradle of true art and true science."

"The most beautiful thing we can experience is the mysterious. It is the source of all true art and science. He to whom the emotion is a stranger, who can no longer pause to wonder and stand wrapped in awe, is as good as dead — his eyes are closed. The insight into the mystery of life, coupled though it be with fear, has also given rise to religion. To know what is impenetrable to us really exists, manifesting itself as the highest wisdom and the most radiant beauty, which our dull faculties can comprehend only in their most primitive forms — this knowledge, this feeling is at the center of true religiousness."

"The most important human endeavor is the striving for morality in our actions. Our inner balance and even our very existence depend on it. Only morality in our actions can give beauty and dignity to life. "

"The most important question a person can ask is, "Is the Universe a friendly place?"

"The most incomprehensible thing about the world is that it is at all comprehensible."

"The only escape from the miseries of life are music and cats..."

"The only real valuable thing is intuition."

"The only source of knowledge is experience."

"The only sure way to avoid making mistakes is to have no new ideas."

"The only thing that interferes with my learning is my education."

"The only thing that you absolutely have to know, is the location of the library."

"The pursuit of truth and beauty is a sphere of activity in which we are permitted to remain children all our lives."

"The release of atomic power has changed everything except our way of thinking ... the solution to this problem lies in the heart of mankind. If only I had known, I should have become a watchmaker. (1945)"

"The Revolution introduced me to art, and in turn, art introduced me to the Revolution!"

"The tragedy of life is what dies inside a man while he lives."

"The true sign of intelligence is not knowledge but imagination."

"The true value of a human being can be found in the degree to which he has attained liberation from the self."

"The woman who follows the crowd will usually go no further than the crowd. The woman who walks alone is likely to find herself in places no one has ever been before."

"The word 'God' is for me nothing more than the expression and product of human weaknesses, and religious scripture a collection of honourable, but still primitive legends which are nevertheless pretty childish. No interpretation, no matter how subtle, can (for me) change this."

"The world as we have created it is a process of our thinking. It cannot be changed without changing our thinking."

"The world is a dangerous place to live, not because of the people who are evil, but because of the people who don't do anything about it."

"There are only two ways to live your life. One is as though nothing is a miracle. The other is as though everything is a miracle."

"There is nothing known as "Perfect". Its only those imperfections which we choose not to see!!"

"Three great forces rule the world: stupidity, fear and greed."

"Time is an illusion."

"To dwell on the things that depress or anger us does not help in overcoming them. One must knock them down alone."

"To punish me for my contempt for authority, fate made me an authority myself."

"Truth is what stands the test of experience. "

"Try not to become a man of success. Rather become a man of value."

"We all know that light travels faster than sound. That's why certain people appear bright until you hear them speak."

"We are all life trying to live, among other life trying to live."

"We are in the position of a little child entering a huge library, whose walls are covered to the ceiling with books in many different languages. The child knows that someone must have written those books. It does not know who or how. It does not understand the the languages in which they are written. The child notes a definite plan in the arrangement of the books, a mysterious order, which it does not comprehend but only dimly suspects."

"We can not solve our problems with the same level of thinking that created them"

"We dance for laughter, we dance for tears, we dance for madness, we dance for fears, we dance for hopes, we dance for screams, we are the dancers, we create the dreams."

"We know from daily life that we exist for other people first of all, for whose smiles and well-being our own happiness depends."

"We should take care not to make the intellect our god; it has, of course, powerful muscles, but no personality. "

"Weakness of attitude becomes weakness of character."

"What a sad era when it is easier to smash an atom than a prejudice."

"What I see in Nature is a magnificent structure that we can comprehend only very imperfectly, and that must fill a thinking person with a feeling of humility. This is a genuinely religious feeling that has nothing to do with mysticism."

"What is right is not always popular and what is popular is not always right."

"What really interests me is whether God had any choice in the creation of the World."

"When I examine myself and my methods of thought, I come to the conclusion that the gift of fantasy has meant more to me than any talent for abstract, positive thinking."

"When the solution is simple, God is answering."

"When you are courting a nice girl an hour seems like a second. When you sit on a red-hot cinder a second seems like an hour. That's relativity."

"When you trip over love, it is easy to get up. But when you fall in love, it is impossible to stand again."

"Whoever is careless with the truth in small matters cannot be trusted with important matters"

"Wisdom is not a product of schooling but of the lifelong attempt to acquire it."

"You can never solve a problem on the level on which it was created."

"You cannot simultaneously prevent and prepare for war."

"You do not really understand something unless you can explain it to your grandmother."

"You have to learn the rules of the game. And then you have to play better than anyone else."

"You never fail until you stop trying."

"You see, wire telegraph is a kind of a very, very long cat. You pull his tail in New York and his head is meowing in Los Angeles. Do you understand this? And radio operates exactly the same way: you send signals here, they receive them there. The only difference is that there is no cat."

Some Facts about Albert Einstein

His father is Hermann Einstein (1847-1902), and his mother Pauline Einstein, née Koch (1858-1920), both came from Jewish families who had lived in the Swabian region for centuries.

Hermann Einstein came from the small town of Buchau in Upper Swabia, where there had been an important Jewish community within the territory of the women's monastery Buchau since the Middle Ages.

Albert Einstein's ancestor, Baruch Moses Einstein, a horse and cloth trader from the Lake Constance region, was the first to be recorded by name and admitted to the community in the 17th century.

The gravestones of the Buchau Jewish cemetery still bear the names of many of Einstein's relatives, including Siegbert Einstein, who survived the Theresienstadt concentration camp and was temporarily the second mayor of Buchau after the Second World War.

Hermann Einstein and his brothers moved to Ulm in 1869. There he married Pauline Koch in 1876 and lived in Bahnhofstraße B135, where Albert Einstein was born on March 14, 1879.

Albert grew up in an assimilated, not strictly believing German-Jewish middle-class family.

Einstein later, shortly after his 50th birthday, spoke to the Ulmer Abendpost about his native town as follows: "The city of birth is just as unique to life as its origin from biological mother. We also owe a part of our being to the city of birth. So I remember Ulm in gratitude because it combines noble artistic tradition with simple and healthy nature."

Albert Einstein kept in touch with his cousin Lina Einstein, who lived in Ulm and was only a little older. In 1940, at the age of 65, she was forcibly admitted to the Jewish old people's home in Oberstotzingen. Albert's attempts to obtain Lina an exit permit to the USA failed. In 1942 Lina Einstein was deported to the Theresienstadt concentration camp and murdered in the same year in the Treblinka extermination camp.

Shortly after Albert's birth in 1880, the family moved to Munich, where his father and uncle founded a small gas and water installation business in October 1880. In 1885 they decided to set up their own factory for electrical equipment (Elektrotechnische Fabrik J. Einstein & Cie) with the support of the entire family.

His father's company was successful and supplied power plants in Munich-Schwabing, Varese, and Susa (Italy).

His sister Maja was born two and a half years after Albert (November 18, 1881, in Munich - June 25, 1951, in Princeton, New Jersey, USA).

His family lived in a building in the backyard of Adlzreiterstrasse 12, which today belongs to the Lindwurmstrasse 127 estate in the Isarvorstadt district of Munich.

Albert Einstein began to speak at the age of three.

At school, he was sometimes even rebellious pupil. His achievements were good to very good, less good in languages, but outstanding in science. Einstein read popular science books and gained an overview of the state of research. In particular, Aaron Bernstein's Volksbücher in the natural sciences are regarded as formative for his interest and further career.

He began playing the violin in 1884 and received private lessons.

In 1885 he went to elementary school, from 1888 he attended the Luitpold-Gymnasium.

The father's company was closed, and the family moved to Milan in 1894. The fifteen-year-old Albert was to remain at the Luitpold-Gymnasium, but was insulted by the director and came into conflict with the school system of the German Empire, which was characterized by discipline and order. Teachers accused him of disrespect off on his classmates. At the end of 1894, Einstein defiantly decided to leave school without graduation and follow his family to Milan.

Another motive might have been to escape the army service. If Einstein had stayed in Germany until the age of 17, he would have been called up for military service - a prospect that frightened him.

In the spring and summer of 1895, Einstein stayed in Pavia, where his parents lived temporarily, and helped out in the company. He made excursions to the Alps and the Apennines and visited his uncle, Julius Koch in Genoa. During this time the 16-year-old Einstein wrote his first scientific paper, an essay entitled Über die Untersuchung des Ätherzustandes im magnetischen Felde, and sent it to his uncle Caesar Koch (1854-1941), who lived in Belgium, for examination. The work was never published as a scientific contribution in a journal and remained in the form of a discussion paper.

Einstein did not comply with his father's wish to study electrical engineering. Instead, he followed the advice of a friend of his family and applied for a place at the Swiss Federal Polytechnic School in Zurich, now ETH Zurich. Since he did not yet have an Abitur or Swiss Matura, he had to take an entrance examination in October 1895, which he - as the youngest participant at the age of 16 - did not pass. He failed due to a lack of knowledge of French.

At the mediation of Albin Herzog, a professor of mechanical engineering, he then attended the liberal cantonal school in Aargau, Switzerland, where he obtained his Matura. During this time in Aarau, he stayed with the Winteler family.

At the beginning of 1896, Einstein gave up his German citizenship and at the same time was registered as not belonging to any religious community. He remained stateless for the next five years.

Einstein's "Maturitätsprüfung" certificate, issued on October 3, 1896, was awarded five times the highest possible grade. The rumor that Einstein was a bad student is wrong: it goes back to Einstein's first biographer, who confused the grading system of Switzerland with that of Germany.

After completing his Matura at the Kantonsschule Aarau, Einstein began his studies at the Polytechnikum Zürich (today ETH Zürich) at the beginning of the academic year 1896.

With his individuality, he often scandalized. The abstract mathematical education was a bad thing in his opinion; he regarded it as a hindrance for the problem-oriented physicist. In the lectures, he attracted the attention of the teaching professor above all by his absence. For the examinations, he relied on the transcripts of his fellow students. This ignorance not only denied him career opportunities at his university, but he also regretted that late in the development of the mathematically highly demanding general Theory of relativity. His fellow student Marcel Grossmann was of great help to him later.

Einstein left the university in 1900 with a diploma as a subject teacher in a mathematic.

His applications for assistant positions at the Polytechnic and other universities were rejected.

He worked as a tutor in Winterthur, Schaffhausen and finally in Bern.

In 1901 his application for Swiss citizenship was granted.

On June 16, 1902, on the recommendation of his friend Marcel Grossmann, Einstein finally obtained a permanent position as a technical expert in 3rd class at the Swiss Patent Office in Bern.

During his studies, Einstein had met his fellow student and later wife, Mileva Marić from Novi Sad. After the death of his father at the end of 1902, the two married in Bern on January 6, 1903 - against the will of the families.

With Marić, Einstein had two sons, Hans Albert (1904-1973) and Eduard (1910-1965). The marriage was divorced in 1919.

In 1987 it became known through the publication of Einstein's letters to Marić from the years 1897 to 1903 that Marić had already born their daughter, called Lieserl, in Novi Sad in January 1902. Nothing is known about the girl's fate; her parents concealed her existence. She may have died of scarlet fever in 1903 or been given up for adoption.

From October 1903 to May 1905, Einstein and Marić lived in the old town of Bern at Kramgasse 49, today's Einsteinhaus Bern, which houses a museum.

In 1905, at the age of 26, Einstein published some of his most important works. The year 1905 was thus an extremely fruitful year, Einstein also speaks of the Annus mirabilis (miracle year). Carl Friedrich von Weizsäcker wrote about this later: "1905 an explosion of genius. Four publications on different topics, each of which, as we say today, is worthy of a Nobel prize."

When Einstein embarked on the long journey from his Theory of special to general relativity in 1907, he was still a largely unknown employee at the Bern Patent Office. At the end of the road, in 1915, he was a professor in Berlin who was already highly regarded among experts and who, as Planck later said, could only be "measured by the achievements of Johannes Kepler and Isaac Newton."

The path to the Theory of general relativity began in 1907 with the flash of inspiration, which Einstein described as "the happiest thought of my life." The flash of inspiration, on the other hand, concerned the equivalence between inertial and heavy mass, i.e. the correspondence between the constant acceleration of a reference system and gravity: "I was sitting on my chair in the Bern Patent Office when suddenly the following thought occurred to me: 'If a person is in free fall, he does not feel his own weight'. I was amazed. This simple thought made a deep impression on me. He drove me towards a theory of gravity".

Einstein's application for a habilitation at Bern University in 1907 was initially rejected, but it was not until the following year that he was successful. In 1909 he was appointed a lecturer in theoretical physics at the University of Zurich.

In January 1911, as Minister of Education Stürgkh announced, he was appointed a full professor of theoretical physics at the German University of Prague. He thus became an Austrian citizen.

In 1913 Max Planck succeeded in winning Einstein as a full-time member of the Prussian Academy of Sciences in Berlin, where he arrived on April 1914. His wife accompanied him with his children but soon returned to Zurich because of private differences. Einstein received his teaching license at Berlin University, but without any obligation to do so.

Freed from all teaching activities, Einstein found time and peace in Berlin to complete his great work, the general Theory of relativity. He was able to publish it in 1916, together with a paper on the Einstein-de-Haas effect.

On October 1, 1917, he became director of the Kaiser Wilhelm Institute for Physics and remained in this position until 1933.

From 1923 to 1933 Einstein was also a member of the Senate of the Kaiser Wilhelm Society.

Between 1917 and 1920 his cousin Elsa Löwenthal (née Einstein; 1876-1936) developed a romantic relationship with him. He divorced Mileva at the beginning of 1919 and married Elsa shortly afterward. She brought two daughters into the marriage.

His mother fell seriously ill at the beginning of 1919 and died the following year.

His Berlin years were marked by active contact with Max Wertheimer, the founder of Gestalt theory. There was a fruitful exchange between the two scientists. Einstein wrote an introduction to Wertheimer's essays on truth, freedom, democracy, and ethics.

Albert Einstein was awarded the 1921 Nobel Prize in Physics on November 9, 1922 "in particular for his discovery of the law of the photoelectric effect."

Einstein left the Nobel Prize money to Mileva Marić and their sons.

On the occasion of Einstein's 50th birthday in 1929, the city of Berlin felt challenged to present its famous citizen with an appropriate gift. Mayor Gustav Böß suggested gifted him a house. The press took up the story. Over time, however, the discussion expanded into an open controversy. Einstein and Elsa, meanwhile searching for a suitable plot of land in Waldstraße in the village of Caputh near Potsdam, found what they were looking for, renounced the gift and financed the house out of their own pockets. The architect Konrad Wachsmann was commissioned to build the modest wooden house on the lake.

This house was the starting point for many tours with the sailing boat during the summer months until 1932. The boat, a birthday present from friends, was confiscated 1933 with Einstein's remaining possessions by the National Socialists.

At the sixth Solvay Conference in 1930, Albert Einstein confronted Niels Bohr surprisingly with his thought experiment of the photon balance, with which he wanted to prove the incompleteness of quantum theory. Only one day later, however, Bohr, together with Pauli and Heisenberg, was able to refute Einstein's argument by considering general relativity.

In 1921 he made his first trip to the USA, where he stayed for several months. He was awarded numerous honorary doctorates, including that of Princeton University, where he was later to teach. Soon he planned to spend half of the year in Princeton, New Jersey, the other half in Berlin. In Berlin, he had become the subject of political debate increasingly because of his pacifist attitude. In December 1932 he traveled again to Pasadena (California).

Einstein traveled to Europe in March/April 1933 after the Nazi regime took power (January 30, 1933); he returned his passport to the German embassy in Brussels.

He informed the Prussian Academy of Sciences, to which he had belonged for 19 years, in writing (with regret) on March 28, 1933, of his resignation. This preceded an expulsion which became apparent after the publication of a pacifist declaration not intended for the press. On April 4, 1933, Einstein filed an application for expatriation. The application was rejected; his citizenship was revoked by expatriation (on March 24, 1934), and he was placed on the second expatriation list from the German Reich.

On May 10, 1933, Propaganda Minister Joseph Goebbels proclaimed: "Jewish intellectualism is dead" and within the framework of the public burning of "undeutschen Schrifttums" symbolically also had Einstein's writings burned. Einstein also found out that his name was on an assassination list with a bounty of 5000 dollars. A German magazine put his name on a list of the enemies of the German nation with the comment: "not yet hanged."

In 1933 Einstein became a member of the Institute for Advanced Study, a private research institute recently founded near Princeton University.

From August 1935 until his death, Einstein lived at 112 Mercer Street in Princeton. The city was then a microcosm of modern research. Einstein soon began searching for a unified field theory that would unite his field theory of gravitation (general relativity) with that of electromagnetism.

In 1936 Einstein's wife Elsa died.

In 1939 his sister Maja came to Princeton - but without her husband Paul, who had not received an entry permit. She lived with her brother until her death in 1951.

In 1938, together with Thomas Mann, he helped the writer Hermann Broch, who had been imprisoned for a short time in Austria, to emigrate to the United States. Both remained friends in exile. Like him, Einstein also helped architect Konrad Wachsmann and numerous other threatened Jewish artists and scientists to leave Germany and enter the USA through letters of recommendation and expert opinions.

On December 15, 1938, he resigned from the Accademia Nazionale dei Lincei in Rome after the latter had expelled all 27 Jewish Italian members.

On October 1, 1940, Einstein received the American citizenship certificate from Judge Phillip Forman.

He retained Swiss citizenship (Zurich) throughout his life.

The discovery of nuclear fission in December 1938 by Otto Hahn and Fritz Straßmann in Berlin conjured up the realization of a nuclear threat in the scientific community. In August 1939, shortly before the beginning of World War II, Einstein signed a letter written by Leó Szilárd to the American President Franklin D. Roosevelt, who warned of the danger of a "bomb of a new type" that Germany might develop and even soon possess. In view of intelligence reports of corresponding German efforts, the appeal was heard, and additional research funds were made available: The Manhattan project with the declared goal of developing an atomic bomb was launched.

In his memoirs, Einstein takes the view that he was too easily convinced of the necessity of signing this letter. On November 16, 1954, he said to his old friend Linus Pauling: "I made one great mistake in my life - when I signed the letter to President Roosevelt recommending that atom bombs be made; but there was some justification - the danger that the Germans would make the bombs."

However, Einstein was completely uninvolved in the works on the Manhattan Project. He was asked by Vannevar Bush in December 1941 for advice on a problem related to isotope separation, but was classified as a security risk by the FBI and official bodies in Washington, partly because of his undisguised sympathies for communism, and was observed by the US secret services. He was therefore not allowed to be officially briefed on the technical details of the Manhattan Project and was even not allowed to know the existence of the top-secret project officially.

As a contribution to the war effort, he donated his original manuscript on the Special Theory of Relativity of 1905, which was auctioned in Kansas City on February 1944 for 6.5 million US dollars invested in US war bonds.

In 1945 Leó Szilárd approached him again, this time to prevent the use of nuclear weapons after Germany's surrender, and Einstein wrote a letter of recommendation for Szilárd to President Roosevelt, which had no consequences because of Roosevelt's death.

After the atomic bomb was dropped, Einstein, who was initially silent, was urged to comment after his 1939 letter to Roosevelt had become known through the Smyth Report. In an interview with a New York Times journalist in September 1945, he spoke out in favor of a world government to prevent wars in the future, came back to this in a Nobel commemorative speech in New York on December 1946.

About his own participation in the initiation of the Manhattan project, he judged in March 1947 in a Newsweek interview that he would not have done so if he had known of the Germans' limited progress in their atomic bomb project, and that the development would also have taken place without him.

He was frequently asked for comments and visited by high state guests such as Jawaharlal Nehru.

Even after his retirement in 1946, he continued to work with assistants at the Institute for Advanced Study on his unified field theory.

His last years were clouded by the death of his sister Maja in 1951 and other friends.

In May 1953, in a letter published in the New York Times, he took a stand against the McCarthy committees and called for refusal to testify.

In 1954 he supported Robert Oppenheimer in his security hearings.

For Einstein, the annihilation of the Jews by Germans during the National Socialist era was the reason for maintaining the general rejection of Arnold Sommerfeld's letter of December 1945 until the end of his life: "After the Germans murdered my Jewish brothers in Europe, I no longer want anything to do with Germans, not even with a relatively harmless academy".

Even years after the war, he saw no pronounced sense of repentance or guilt in Germany and continued to avoid any involvement with the public institutions there. He rejected a request by Otto Hahn to become a member of the Max Planck Society with just as clear a voice as that of Sommerfeld to reinstate him in the Bavarian Academy of Sciences, or that of Theodor Heuss with regard to the Order of Pour le Mérite. Nor did he want his books to appear in Germany in future. He reacted with incomprehension to the news that his friend Max Born wanted to move back to Germany. However, he did not generally transfer his dislike of Germany to individuals or colleagues, especially if, like Sommerfeld, Max Planck, and Max von Laue, they had kept their distance from the Nazis.

On April 11, 1955, together with ten other renowned scientists, he signed the so-called Russell Einstein Manifesto to Raise People's Awareness of Disarmament.

Einstein's final notes concern a speech he wanted to make on the anniversary of Israeli independence. On April 13, 1955, he worked on the draft together with the Israeli consul. In the afternoon of the same day, Einstein collapsed and was taken to Princeton Hospital two days later.

Einstein died on April 18, 1955, at the age of 76 in Princeton from internal bleeding caused by the rupture of an aneurysm in the aorta.

Einstein had been suffering from the aneurysm for years. It was discovered at the end of 1948. Due to health problems he had hardly left Princeton since the end of the 1940s.

The night nurse Alberta Roszel of Princeton Hospital was with Einstein when he died. She reported that shortly before his death, he had muttered something in German.

The pathologist Thomas Harvey took Albert Einstein's brain and eyes after the autopsy. His intention was above all to preserve the brain for further investigation of its possibly unique structure for posterity. Most of the brain is now preserved in the National Museum of Health and Medicine in Chicago, the eyes in New York.

According to Einstein's wish, his body was burned and the ashes scattered in an unknown place.

Einstein had been proposed for the Nobel Prize from 1910 with increasing frequency, especially from 1919. However, this met with persistent resistance in the Nobel Prize Committee, which also led to the fact that the 1921 Prize was not awarded on time, but only one year later together with the 1922 Prize.

A famous discussion connects Einstein with the physicist Niels Bohr. The subject was the different interpretations of the new quantum theory which Heisenberg, Schrödinger, and Dirac developed from 1925. Einstein was particularly critical of the concept of Bohr. Einstein believed that the random elements of quantum theory would later be proven and they are to be not really random. This attitude led him, for the first time in a dispute with Max Born, to the famous statement that the old man (or Lord) did not throw dice: "Anyway, I'm convinced that the old man doesn't roll the dice."

In his late years, Einstein dealt with the question of a unified field theory of all forces of nature-based on his general Theory of relativity; an undertaking which, however, was not crowned with success and is still unsolved today.

Einstein contributed to the technique of the gyrocompass with his inventions of the electrodynamics drive for the gyroscopes. Einstein had acquired relevant specialist knowledge in 1914 when he was appointed an expert in a patent dispute between Hermann Anschütz-Kaempfe and Elmer Ambrose Sperry. Mechanical gyro compasses are still built today using Einstein's patented technology.

Presumably inspired by Ludwig Hopf, Einstein studied the flow properties of aircraft wings at the beginning of the First World War and designed a wing profile around 1916 in which he wanted to reduce air resistance by dispensing with the angle of attack. In August 1916 he published the work Elementary Theory of Water Waves and Flight. The airline in Berlin-Johannisthal implemented Einstein's design proposals, and the wings were called cat's hump wings because of their less than elegant shape. However, a test flight showed that the construction was unusable due to its poor flight characteristics. The test pilot Paul G. Ehrhardt had had great difficulty landing the plane again and described it as a "pregnant duck." Einstein himself was later, probably also in view of possible military applications, glad that his suggestions had proved to be useless, and was ashamed of his "foolishness from those days."

Already at the age of nineteen, Einstein felt such disgust for militarism that he gave up his German citizenship.

The beginning of the First World War led to an intensive engagement with political problems. Einstein joined the Bund Neues Vaterland (the later German League for Human Rights) and supported its demands for an early, just peace without territorial demands and the creation of an international organization to prevent future wars.

In 1918 Albert Einstein was one of the signatories of the call to found the left-liberal German Democratic Party (DDP). In the course of the Weimar Republic, he continued to be involved in the German League for Human Rights, in which he stood up for political prisoners.

In 1932 he signed the Urgent Appeal together with Heinrich Mann, Ernst Toller, Käthe Kollwitz, Arnold Zweig, and others for an anti-fascist left alliance of SPD, KPD and trade unions to prevent the downfall of the Weimar Republic and the threatening of National Socialism.

From 1922 he was a member of the Commission for Spiritual Cooperation of the then League of Nations, at whose suggestion he later entered into an exchange of letters with Sigmund Freud in September 1932 on the question Why War? which was published in 1933.

In 1931, together with Heinrich Mann, he drew attention to the murder of the Croatian intellectual Milan Šufflay in an open letter to the New York Times.

At the beginning of March 1933, during a stay in the USA, he left a statement to the League for the Fight against Anti-Semitism.

Einstein also opposed violence against animals and sympathized with the idea of vegetarianism. But it was probably only towards the end of his life that he probably fed himself a vegetarian diet.

Affected by the situation of Eastern European Jewish refugees after the First World War, Einstein showed increased commitment to an Israeli state. In 1918 his participation in a provisional committee for the preparation of a Jewish congress in Germany was documented.

He largely supported the Zionist ideals, but never joined a Zionist organization.

His name is strongly associated with the Hebrew University in Jerusalem. One of the purposes of his first trip to the USA was to collect donations for such a university. In 1923 he traveled to Palestine to lay the foundation stone - during this trip, he was awarded the first honorary citizenship of the city of Tel Aviv. In 1925 he was appointed a member of the university's board of directors. Finally, in his will, Einstein ordered the transfer of his written estate to the Hebrew University.

After the death of Chaim Weizmann in 1952, Einstein received the offer to become the second president of the newly founded state of Israel, which he rejected, however.

In December 1982, the Hebrew University in Jerusalem received Albert Einstein's private archive. The material dates from 1901 to 1955 and comprises 50,000 pages and about 33 unpublished manuscripts until 1982.

Einstein wrote his little-known essay Why Socialism? in 1949, in which he set out his political position: Although he admits not to be an expert in the field of economics, he considers a statement admissible.

He criticized capitalism for failing to meet society's economic needs: "Production is there for profit - not for demand. There is no provision for all those who are able and willing to work always to be able to find work". But he also demanded that the desired socialism must respect the rights of the individual: "A planned economy as such can go hand in hand with the total enslavement of the individual. Socialism requires the solution of some extremely difficult socio-political problems: Given the far-reaching centralization of political and economic forces, how is it possible to prevent bureaucracy from becoming omnipotent and excessive? How can the rights of the individual be protected, thereby ensuring a democratic counterweight to bureaucracy? [...] Clarity about the aims and problems of socialism is of the utmost importance in our time of transition. Unfortunately, in the present state of society, a powerful taboo makes it difficult to discuss these things freely."

In the U.S., Einstein was under FBI surveillance for his political views. Agents not only tapped his phone and checked his mail, but also searched the garbage. The FBI file with so-called "incriminating information" against Einstein comprises a total of 1800 pages.

Until the 21st century, there are various interpretations of Einstein's attitude to religion, as he often expressed himself contradictorily, among other things with the aphorism: "Science without religion is lame, religion without science is blind." He clearly distances himself from the biblical idea of a personal God, which he calls "childlike superstition": "I have said several times that in my opinion, the idea of a personal God is a childlike one, [...]. You can call me an agnostic, but I don't share the fighting spirit of a professional atheist ... I prefer a humble attitude regarding the weakness of our intellectual understanding of nature and being."

Printed in Great Britain
by Amazon